Facts About the Cow

By Lisa Strattin

© 2019 Lisa Strattin

Facts for Kids Picture Books by Lisa Strattin

Harlequin Macaw, Vol 34

Downy Woodpecker, Vol 37

Frilled Lizard, Vol 39

Purple Finch, Vol 48

Poison Dart Frogs, Vol 50

Giant Otter, Vol 57

Hornbill, Vol 67

Dwarf Lemur, Vol 73

Giant Squirrel, Vol 76

Star Tortoise, Vol 79

Sign Up for New Release Emails Here

http://LisaStrattin.com/subscribe-here

Monthly Surprise Box

http://KidCraftsByLisa.com

Contents

INTRODUCTION

Cows are raised in many different countries around the world, mainly for the cow's natural resources such as milk, meat and leather. In India, the cow is seen as a sacred animal.

There are thought to be nearly 1.5 million cows worldwide, most of the cows are kept by farmers but there is sure to be the odd escaped wild cow occasionally!

It is commonly thought that male cows, called bulls, are aggravated by the color red. This is in fact not true as cows and bulls are color blind and cannot distinguish between different colours, as far as scientists tell us. This common misconception has come about from the days of bull fighting where matadors, bull fighters, were typically seen waving a red flag at them. It is not the color of the flag that would spur the bull on but in fact, the waving of the flag itself.

CHARACTERISTICS

Cows spend their days in herds of around 40-50 cows, grazing on the grasslands and shrubbery. There is an old English tale which claims that cows will always sit down when it's going to rain.

The cow is known well amongst farmers for its ability to interbreed with species that are closely related to the cow. These can include yaks and bison, where these animals have been successfully bred with the cow to produce hybrid cattle. Oddly enough though, the cow is unable to successfully breed with buffalo or the water buffalo.

The cow has just one stomach (not four) but the cow's stomach contains four separate compartments that work with the complex digestive system of the cow which allows the cow to control substances that are difficult and near impossible for many other animals to digest.

APPEARANCE

There are many different varieties of cows, and they are many colors. There are light and dark brown cows, white with brown spots and white with black spots as well as the other way around! Some are kept by farmers for their milk, others are raised for the beef we eat. Hamburgers and steaks are usually from beef, although lots of people also eat burgers made of other meat too.

The leather we get for our belts and cowboy boots are made from the cow hide. We get lots of the things we use every day from the cow!

LIFE STAGES

A cow that has never had a baby is called a heifer. Their babies are called calves and they are born live. They can stand soon after birth and nurse from their mother's milk until they are old enough to eat grasses. The mother cow is usually around 2 years old when she has her first calf.

LIFE SPAN

Cows usually live from 12 to 20 years. It is unknown how long they might live in the wild, since most of the cows we know of are kept by farmers and ranchers.

SIZE

Most cows and bulls are 5 to 6 feet tall and weigh between 800 to 1700 pounds. The bulls tend to weigh more than the cows and are very large animals!

HABITAT

Cows thrive in herds kept and cared for by farmers and ranchers. The size of the herd depends completely on how many the farmer has, but in general terms, a cow will stay in a herd of around 50 animals or so.

Bulls, on the other hand, are usually kept to themselves. They stay in a pasture area just for them, unless they are with a cow during breeding season. They are territorial and will not run from a challenge.

DIET

Cows and bulls are herbivores. They eat grasses, seeds, flowers and hay. Farmers provide good quality grasses and hay for their animals in order to keep them healthy and strong.

FRIENDS AND ENEMIES

People are both friends and enemies to these animals. Farmers and ranchers take good care of them, but then they take them "to market" to sell for their meat and hide. Dairy cows are not used for meat, they are kept only for their milk, so people are truly friends to them.

Bears and wolves are known to attack these animals, so they are predatory enemies.

SUITABILITY AS PETS

A cow can become very tame and comfortable around humans. You can also get to know a cow and their personality. Even though you won't want one in your house, a cow can be treated as a pet as long as you leave it outside in a pasture.

A bull is not so easy, though. They tend to become agitated easily, and they like to be left alone, so it's not too likely that you can make a "pet" out of a bull.

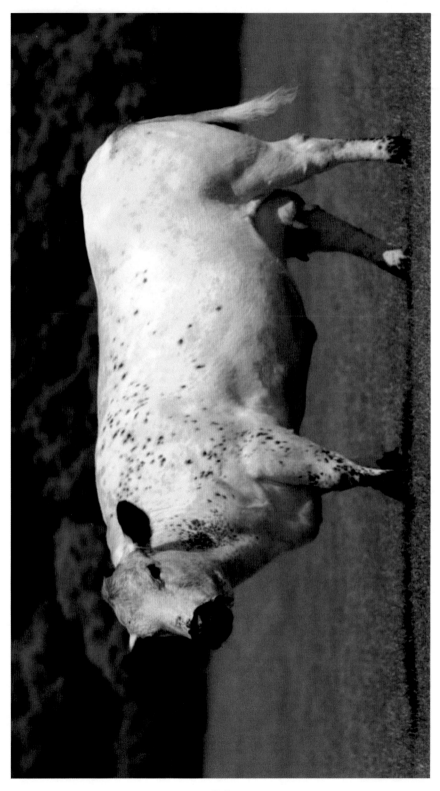

COLOR ME

COLOR ME

COLOR ME

COLOR ME

COLOR ME

COLOR ME

COLOR ME

COLOR ME

COLOR ME

Please leave me a review here:

http://lisastrattin.com/Review-Vol-180

For more Kindle Downloads Visit Lisa Strattin Author Page on Amazon Author Central

http://amazon.com/author/lisastrattin

To see upcoming titles, visit my website at LisaStrattin.com– all books available on kindle!

http://lisastrattin.com

PLUSH COW TOY

You can get one by copying and pasting this link into your browser:

http://lisastrattin.com/PlushCow

MONTHLY SURPRISE BOX

Get yours by copying and pasting this link into your browser

http://KidCraftsByLisa.com

Made in United States
Orlando, FL
27 November 2021